Mythical Creatures

UNICORNS

Martha London

DiscoverRoo
An Imprint of Pop!
popbooksonline.com

abdobooks.com

Published by Pop!, a division of ABDO, PO Box 398166, Minneapolis, Minnesota 55439.

Printed in the United States of America, North Mankato, Minnesota.

102019
012020

THIS BOOK CONTAINS RECYCLED MATERIALS

Cover Photo: Shutterstock Images
Interior Photos: Shutterstock Images, 1, 6, 9, 10, 15 (top left), 17, 18, 24–25, 25; iStockphoto, 5, 11, 13, 14, 15 (top right), 20–21, 23, 26, 27, 29, 31; Red Line Editorial, 12; Rankin/Bass Productions/Photo 12/Alamy, 15 (bottom), 30; Arnold Bocklin/Ivy Close Images/Alamy, 19; Fine Art Images/Heritage Image Partnership Ltd/Alamy, 28

Editor: Sophie Geister-Jones
Series Designer: Jake Nordby

Library of Congress Control Number: 2019942471

Publisher's Cataloging-in-Publication Data

Names: London, Martha, author.

Title: Unicorns / by Martha London

Description: Minneapolis, Minnesota : Pop!, 2020 | Series: Mythical creatures | Includes online resources and index.

Identifiers: ISBN 9781532165818 (lib. bdg.) | ISBN 9781532167133 (ebook)

Subjects: LCSH: Mythical animals--Juvenile literature. | Unicorns--Juvenile literature. | Folklore--Juvenile literature. | Legends--Juvenile literature. | Animals and history--Juvenile literature.

Classification: DDC 398.469--dc23

WELCOME TO DiscoverRoo!

Pop open this book and you'll find QR codes loaded with information, so you can learn even more!

Scan this code* and others like it while you read, or visit the website below to make this book pop!

popbooksonline.com/unicorns

*Scanning QR codes requires a web-enabled smart device with a QR code reader app and a camera.

TABLE OF CONTENTS

CHAPTER 1

A UNICORN'S GIFT

People in the village were getting sick. The water was poisoned. A group went to the woods to look for a river. The people heard a rustling sound. A unicorn stepped out from the trees. His long

WATCH A VIDEO HERE!

Unicorns are very beautiful creatures.

mane sparkled in the sunlight. A white horn stuck out from his forehead.

Many images of unicorns can be found in paintings and tapestries. Tapestries are similar to woven blankets.

The unicorn's horn had magical powers. It could clean the village's water. A girl approached the unicorn. She asked him to save her village. The unicorn bowed to the girl. He followed her back to the village. There, he dipped his horn into the well. The poison disappeared. All the villagers cheered. The unicorn had saved them.

DID YOU KNOW?

Some people believed unicorns had healing powers. They claimed a belt made of unicorn skin could prevent stomachaches.

CHAPTER 2

UNICORNS IN HISTORY

The first pictures of unicorns come from thousands of years ago. These images appeared on coins in East Asia. They showed a large animal. It looked like

LEARN MORE HERE!

Many countries had stories of unicorn-like creatures. In Japan, these animals were called ***kirin.***

a bull. The animal had short legs and the tail of a donkey. Its horn was curved.

A unicorn can also be called a monoceros. This name means "one-horned beast."

Legends about unicorns also existed in Europe. These stories began to be written down in 430 BCE. In early stories, unicorns were colorful. They looked like donkeys. But they had white bodies and purple heads. Their horns were red with black tips.

Another **ancient** writer claimed that unicorns had the feet of an elephant and the head of a deer.

REAL UNICORNS?

Most people no longer believe unicorns exist. But some people claim they are real. One is Oberon Zell. In 1984, Zell found a way to make goats look like unicorns. He **fused** each goat's horns together in the middle of its forehead. He sold one of these goats to a circus. The goat's name was Lancelot.

WHERE DO UNICORNS COME FROM?

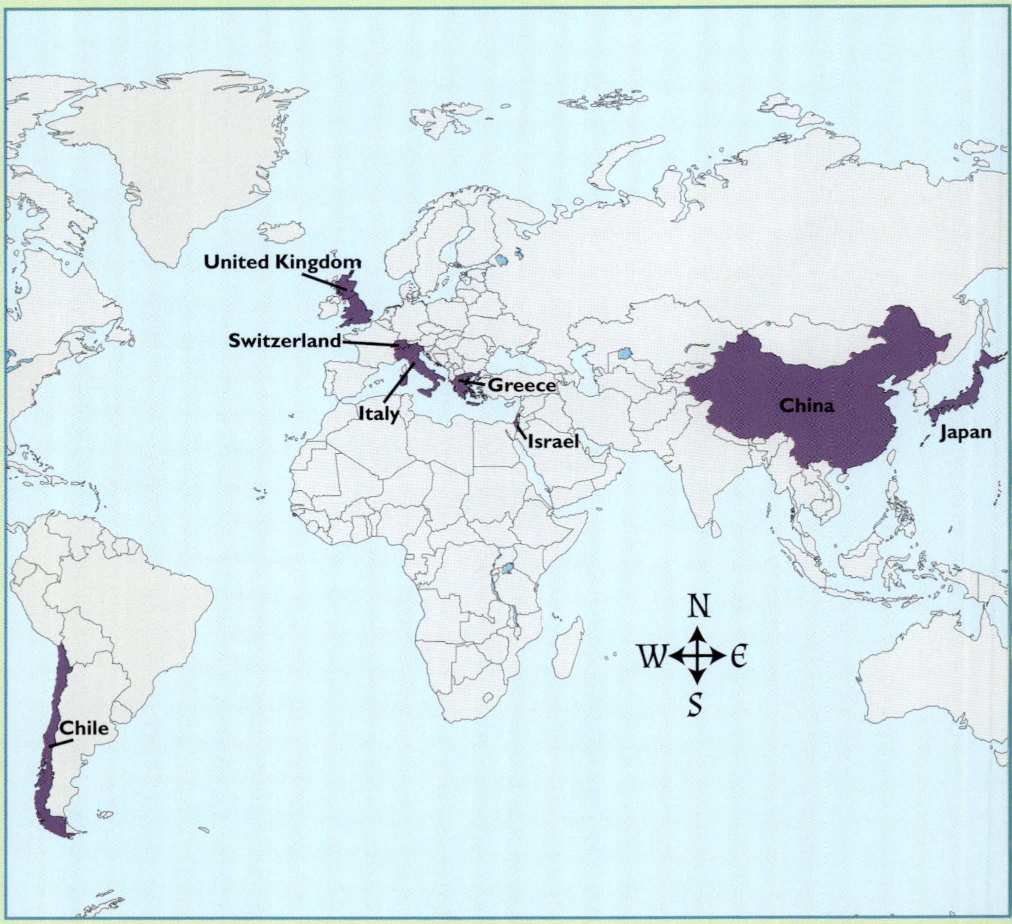

By the **Middle Ages**, however, legends were changing. Unicorns began to look more like they do in stories and movies today.

DID YOU KNOW?

Researchers believe stories of unicorns may have been inspired by rhinoceroses.

UNICORNS THROUGH THE YEARS

430 BCE
Unicorns are first mentioned in a history text by Ctesias.

1200
Kings and queens in Europe begin buying fake unicorn horns from traders.

100 CE
A Greek text called the *Physiologus* describes what unicorns and other mythical creatures look like.

1600
The constellation Monoceros is named. It looks like a unicorn.

2008
A one-horned deer is spotted in Italy. Similar animals may have inspired stories of unicorns.

1982
The movie *The Last Unicorn* is released.

CHAPTER 3

UNICORN LOOKS

In most modern stories, unicorns look like horses with horns in the middle of their heads. But unicorns are sometimes described as a mix between a horse and goat. They can have **cloven** hooves.

COMPLETE AN ACTIVITY HERE!

Unicorn horns are grooved, which make them look like spirals.

Almost all unicorns have white hair, though some are silver. According to **legends**, unicorns glow in the moonlight. They have strong bodies and legs. They can run very fast.

Sometimes, unicorns will let people ride on their backs.

The most famous part of a unicorn is its horn. Legends say unicorn horns are made of alicorn. This material was supposed to have many magical powers. People believed it could protect against

Unicorn horns were once valued more than gold.

poison. Doctors claimed it could **cure** diseases too.

DID YOU KNOW?

One doctor claimed shoes made of unicorn skin prevented the plague. The plague was a deadly illness that killed many people.

CHAPTER 4

UNICORN POWER

Unicorns are known as protectors of other creatures. They are kind and quiet. Some **legends** say unicorns walk so softly that any animal or bug they accidentally step on is unhurt.

LEARN MORE HERE!

Most unicorns live alone. They often live in forests.

In some stories, unicorns grow their horns when they are four years old.

Unicorns are gentle. They do not fight unless they have to. They prefer to run from danger and are very hard to catch. But unicorns will protect any innocent person or animal that needs help.

When they do fight, unicorns are brave and fierce. They kick with their hooves. They bite and stab with their horn. Legends say unicorn horns are sharp. They can pierce any material.

One way to capture a unicorn is to get its horn stuck in a tree.

Because of these behaviors, unicorns are often **symbols** of goodness. Kings and queens used unicorns as models for how to act. They admired how

A unicorn's magic is a gift. It cannot be stolen.

the animals protected innocent people.

Today, stories about unicorns show them as kind and gentle. They continue to capture people's imaginations.

DID YOU KNOW?

The unicorn is Scotland's national animal.

MAKING CONNECTIONS

TEXT-TO-SELF

What would you do if you encountered a unicorn?

TEXT-TO-TEXT

Have you read books about other mythical creatures? How are the legends about those creatures similar to legends about unicorns?

TEXT-TO-WORLD

Unicorns are often symbols of goodness. What is another creature or animal that people use as a symbol? What does it usually represent?

GLOSSARY

ancient – from a long time ago.

cloven – split into two parts.

cure – to heal or end a sickness.

fuse – to combine two or more things using force.

legend – a story passed down over many years.

Middle Ages – the period of European history between the 400s CE and the 1400s CE.

symbol – an animal or object that stands for a feeling or action.

INDEX

ONLINE RESOURCES

popbooksonline.com

Scan this code* and others like it while you read, or visit the website below to make this book pop!

popbooksonline.com/unicorns

*Scanning QR codes requires a web-enabled smart device with a QR code reader app and a camera.